SPAIN
A PICTURE MEMORY

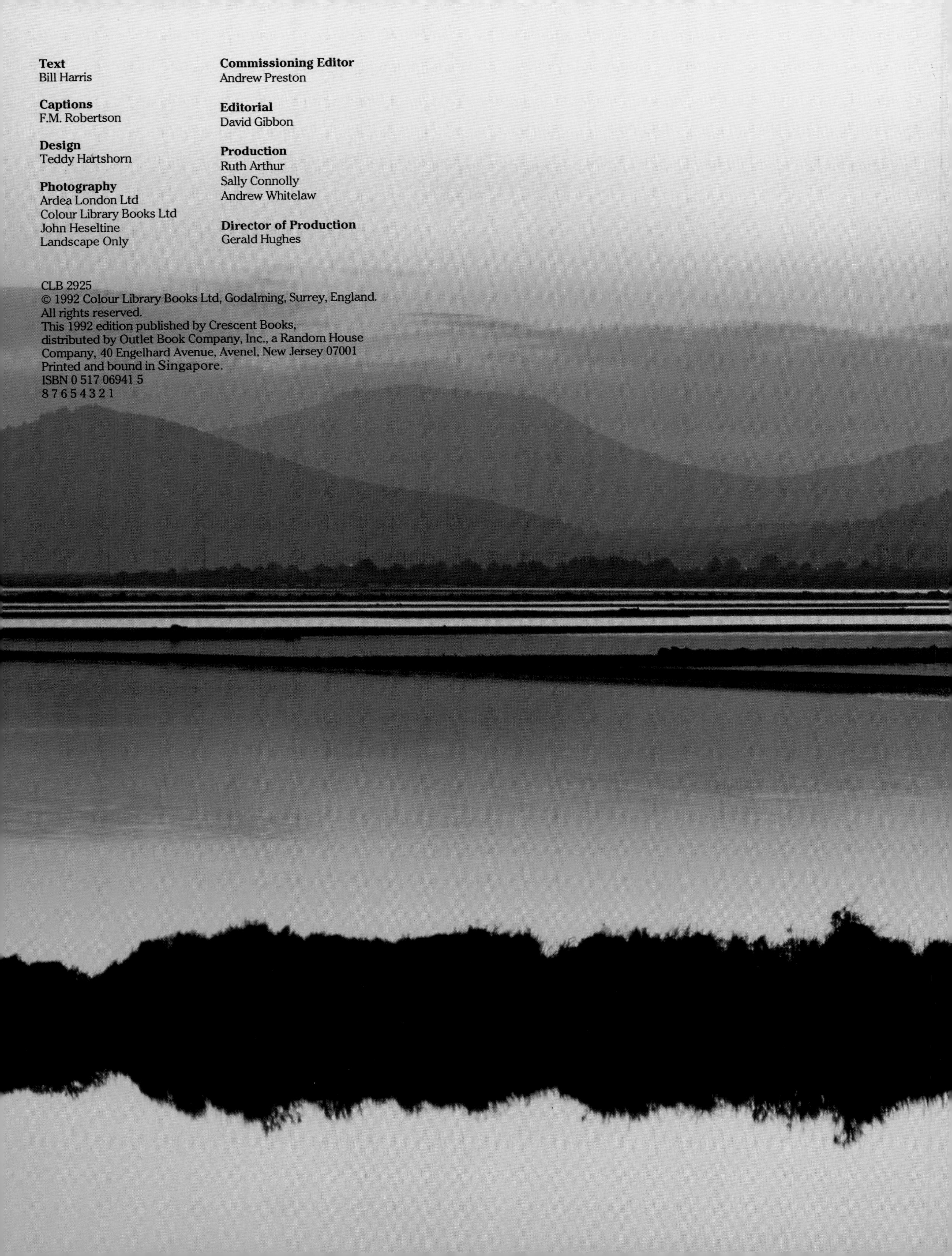

Text
Bill Harris

Captions
F.M. Robertson

Design
Teddy Hartshorn

Photography
Ardea London Ltd
Colour Library Books Ltd
John Heseltine
Landscape Only

Commissioning Editor
Andrew Preston

Editorial
David Gibbon

Production
Ruth Arthur
Sally Connolly
Andrew Whitelaw

Director of Production
Gerald Hughes

SPAIN

A PICTURE MEMORY

CRESCENT BOOKS
NEW YORK • AVENEL, NEW JERSEY

Castles in Spain. Was there ever a trio of words that could conjure up pure romance in quite the same way? There are castles all over Europe, even Walt Disney's kingdom has them, and most of the fortresses that gave the region of Castile its name are based on German and French models. But Spain outdid them all in both romance and solid comfort with the castle of Burgos, which became the setting for the start of one of the great love stories in the history of English royalty.

It was in the year 1254 that the fifteen-year-old boy who would become England's King Edward I went to Burgos to meet his new bride, ten-year-old Eleanor of Castile. After they were married at the Convent of Las Huelgas, they moved to England, where the girl insisted on living in the style she had been accustomed to at the castle of Burgos, which left many Englishmen horrified at the expense but impressed the rest with trappings of luxury none of them had ever dreamed of. Her courtiers hung the walls with silk and tapestries and covered the floors with carpets, ideas that had been taken to Spain by the Moors but until then had never crossed the Pyrenees into the rest of Europe. As she was growing up, Eleanor so bedazzled the English that they made her their queen at the same time her husband was crowned king, and her devotion to Edward and their thirteen children made her Spanish background a thing to be emulated. As she and her husband wandered from castle to castle in England and in the Middle East they took her Spanish/Moorish ideas of comfort with them, and castles everywhere, on the inside at least, began to resemble more and more the castles of Spain.

The fortress that once overlooked Burgos has long since been reduced to a windswept plain, but dozens of others are still standing, and the good news for romantics is that many have become part of the government-run chain of parador hotels. One of them, the 14th-century successor to a Roman fort at Siguenza, near Madrid, was a home-away-from-home for King Ferdinand and Queen Isabella, and in recent years became a favorite of the present King Juan Carlos.

Solid comfort is as important as historic authenticity in the castles and convents that have been converted to five-star hotels in Spain, but history, mercifully, isn't served down to the last detail. Back in the days when Don Quixote was riding through the countryside transforming inns into castles in his mind's eye, his creator, Miguel de Cervantes, described the accommodations in terms of the reality every 17th-century Spanish traveler easily recognized: "Don Quixote's hard, scanty, beggarly and miserable bed was the first of four in that dingy room," he wrote, "next to it was Sancho's kennel, which consisted of nothing but a bed mat and coverlet." Fortunately, the refurbished paradors not only include oversized four-poster beds, but each and every room comes with its own bath, an amenity that in medieval Spain would have been considered an invitation to heresy.

During the Middle Ages, almost no one anywhere in Europe considered bathing anything more than a waste of time, but in Spain it was regarded as both unhealthy and unchristian. During six hundred years of Roman rule, public baths were not only popular, but quite common, but when the Goths drove the Romans out in the fifth century they decided that lolling around in warm water made a man soft and feminine, and they proceeded to dismantle the baths. Then when the Moors took over they were completely fascinated by water in almost direct proportion to the natives' lack of fascination with it. Over time, the Spanish began to equate cleanliness with the religious practices of the Moslems and the Jews who followed them into Spain, and eventually they came to believe that the most important mark of a true Christian was an *olor de santidad*. Monks took great pride in never changing their robes, and when St. Teresa was accidentally dumped into a river she considered it a grim joke perpetrated by Christ, whom she publicly rebuked for the affront. But the record-holder was Princess Isabel who went well over three years without once taking off her dress, scoring a double blow, as it were, for the cause of Christian piety. And a poet of the day could think of no finer way of describing the residents of a convent than as "a sweet garden of flowers, perfumed by the good odor of sanctity."

Christianity survived the fad. So did Spain. Both survived the Inquisition, too, when thousands died for what the authorities claimed was insincerity in their forced conversion to the Catholic faith. The fifteenth-century search for heretics spread to other parts of Europe before it moved from Castile to other regions of Spain, because then, as now, the Spanish are the most individualistic people on the continent. Even though Spanish is spoken by 331 million people, almost ten times the population of Spain itself, and after Mandarin, Hindi and English is the world's most common language, it isn't the principal language in every part of Spain. They don't even call it Spanish there, but prefer it to be known as Castilian. The Basques converse with one another in their ancient language of Euskadi; in Catalonia, the language is Catalan, and Valencia and Galicia each have distinct languages of their own.

The geography of the peninsula is the main culprit. There are mountains everywhere, more of them than in any other part of Europe except Switzerland, and they are rugged enough to have kept the ancestors of today's Spaniards apart throughout all their history. They have even affected the weather. The high central plain that covers the center of the country and the southern coastal area is hot, dry, and, as the travel brochures love to point out, "sunny." But the northwest gets more rainfall than Britain, and there are valleys and bogs there that make it seem more like Ireland than sunny Spain.

The Pyrenees, higher than the Alps in most places, have also kept the Spanish people apart from the rest of Europe, even though Spain's earliest culture was established by Celts who crossed the mountain passes from the north. They were overshadowed by immigrants from northern Africa, who called themselves *Iberians*, which in their language meant "river;" obviously the most impressive feature of the landscape to former desert nomads. The Greeks came along several centuries later, in about 600 B.C., and along with a new name for the peninsula, *Hesperia*, the land of the setting sun, they also planted there the first olives and grapes. The Phoenecians had already been trading along the Mediterranean shores for several hundred years by then, and when the Persians conquered them, they took control of the the city-state of Carthage on the North African coast and through it began to dominate the Iberian Peninsula. They had yet another name for the place, preferring to call it *Ispania*, which to them meant "the land of the rabbits."

The Carthaginians set about developing the resources of the peninsula, founding such great cities as Barcelona and New Carthage, now the seaport of Cartagena. The Romans, meanwhile, were pushing southward from their colonies in Gaul, and when the great general Hannibal took control of the Carthaginian army in 221 B.C., he decided to do something about it. The result was the Second Punic War, during which Hannibal surprised the Romans by leading an army of Iberian mercenaries and the incredible slingshot-armed natives of the Balearic Islands across the Alps into Italy, using elephants as pack animals. But the Roman legions struck back in Spain itself under the leadership of Scipio Africanus, one of the most daring generals Rome had ever produced, who forced the Carthaginians back to North Africa and began to turn Spain into one of most important provinces under Roman control.

The problem was that even the Romans couldn't fuse it into a single province. Their hope was to exploit the natural resources and recruit the locals as mercenary soldiers as the Carthaginians had set out to do, but the locals seemed to prefer fighting against the conquerors rather than for them. The Romans had come up against resistance before, but they had never come up against a people like the Iberians. The professional soldiers were usually able to subdue less civilized people with brute force, and always succeeded when the enemy united against them and could be brought down together in a few large battles. But the Spanish didn't unite against them, preferring to fight in small groups, usually from ambush. The situation continued for two hundred years, alternating between guerilla wars and periods of strained peace until Julius Caesar arrived on the scene in 45 B.C. to defeat the forces of Pompey the Great, who had taken control of the occupation. His victory over the occupiers not only made Caesar a hero among the Iberians, but it made him the uncontested master of Rome itself.

After Caesar's assassination two years later, his successor, Augustus, made Spain his first order of business, and by then the Iberians were ready to adopt the Latin culture as their own. Within a few years, the Roman garrison in Spain was reduced to a single legion, augmented by dozens that were composed entirely of native soldiers. Better still, all citizens of the province were made full citizens of Rome, which united them to each other for the first time in their history. The bond made both Rome and Iberia prosperous, too, and its influence on Spanish culture is still evident, both in the language, which is quite close to the Latin dialect spoken by the Roman soldiers, and the Christian religion, which became the universal faith in Spain, as it did throughout the Empire, after the reign of the Emperor Constantine.

Actually, Christianity came to this corner of the Empire about two hundred years before Constantine's reign. Tradition says that James the Apostle went to Spain in 40 A.D. and stayed for a half-dozen years before returning to Jerusalem, where he was beheaded. His body, according to the story, was returned to Spain and buried near the city that would eventually be named Santiago in his honor. The grave became the object of pilgrimages until Roman oppression of Christians made it a place best avoided, and it was forgotten for almost eight hundred years. It was rediscovered by a hermit who claimed to have been led to the spot by a bright star and the sound of strange music. The discovery was regarded as a miracle by church officials and Santiago, after Rome and Jerusalem, became the holiest spot in Christendom. And the legend eventually gave the Spanish Christians the inspiration they needed to drive the Moslems from the country. Although the Apostle probably never killed anyone in his life, he became revered by the Spanish as *Matamores*, the slayer of Moors.

The Romans and their Spanish allies fell victim to the hordes of Germanic barbarians who poured across the Pyrenees in 409 A.D. They stayed on the scene for three centuries, creating a monarchy to govern themselves and enhancing the role of the church, both as a political power and as an educational force. But they also created an atmosphere of court intrigues. One of them, according to some accounts, set the stage for the next wave of conquerors.

The Moslems were quite a new force in the world at the time. The Prophet Mohammed had been dead less than eighty years when his followers attacked Spain in 711, and although he had commanded them to use fire and sword to carry his teachings into the land of the infidel, they had attempted to storm Iberia twice before and failed. They seem to have decided to concentrate on consolidating their influence in North Africa, and were at war in Mauretania when feuding broke out among pretenders to the Spanish throne. The losers went to Africa, where the commander of

the Goth fortress at Cueta, opposite the Rock of Gibraltar, was apparently willing to help them settle their score with the new king. According to the story, the king had seduced the general's daughter, and he had a score of his own to settle.

It didn't take much to convince the Moors to help, and within seven years, with considerable assistance from some of the Goths themselves, who thought the Moslems had come to help fight their war of succession, almost all of the Iberian Peninsula had become part of the Caliphate of Damascus. The Moslem advance was stopped in Southern France by the forces of Charles Martel twenty years later, but they stayed in Spain for eight hundred years, adding yet another influence to a culture that was already a mixture of Roman, Christian and German traditions.

But the most important tradition of all, a resistance to unification, flowered in Moslem Spain. Mohammed had unified the Arabs under his banner, but transplanted to a new land they went back to fighting among themselves, and their days in Spain were filled with alternating periods of internal warfare. Before they finally left, the country was divided into as many as three dozen separate Moorish kingdoms, and almost as many would-be Christian kings were trying to get their acts together in the north.

Still, in an era when most European countries were struggling through what are remembered as the Dark Ages, culture was flourishing in Spain. Literature, art, architecture and science were not only kept alive, but advanced thanks, in part, to the unprecedented tolerance of the Moslems, who had no problem coexisting with Christians and Jews or even encouraging them to contribute ideas that could benefit them all.

But if the Moors tolerated Christianity, the Christians of Spain never got used to the idea that Islam was the dominant religion in their midst, and there was hardly a moment in eight centuries that the idea of "reconquest" wasn't near the top of the Spanish agenda. The battle lines were drawn at Covadonga in the northern mountains in 722, and although the line wavered over the years, the frontier moved inexorably southward until, by the middle of the thirteenth century, only Granada was still a Moorish kingdom. Most of the gains had been made in a single generation, during which Ferdinand, the heir to the throne of Aragon, married Isabella, the sister of the childless king of Castile. The marriage contract was carefully crafted to let them function as equals, but most important, it was also a marriage of the two kingdoms. Isabella became Castile's Queen in 1474, and five years later, after Ferdinand's succession, they decided to unite all of Spain as a new Christian kingdom. But first the Jews and the Moslems had to be taken care of. The Inquisition was established in 1480 to take care of the Jewish problem, and the following year their Catholic Majesties declared war on the Moors.

The war ended after the long siege of Granada, in 1492, but the Moslems were allowed to stay if they would agree to convert to Christianity. The Jews, on the other hand, were ordered out of the country on pain of death, and more than 150,000 of them followed the order. By the end of the first decade of the 17th century, there were neither Jews nor Moslems, converted or otherwise, in any noticeable numbers anywhere in Spain. The country was unified at last. And it was a solidly Catholic country, ironically emerging in the same era that the Protestant Reformation was beginning to sweep Europe.

Over the centuries that have followed, the Spanish have shared the glories of their civilization with the rest of the world with the same enthusiasm they often seem to have retreated from it. But in recent years, since the death of dictator Francisco Franco in 1975, there is a new spirit abroad in the land. Always considered one of the world's most conservative countries, modern Spain is quickly becoming one of Europe's most liberal. There are topless bathers on some of its beaches, and rock music is almost as common as choral masses in the larger cities.

The new Spain is also evident in the missions of the official visitors who are flocking there these days. Since it became a partner in the European Economic Community, most of them have been businessmen looking for investment opportunities. Those same investors have lately turned their eyes to the new democracies in Central Europe, but they're more likely to find the people they need to talk with in Spain. The leaders responsible for adapting their countries to free market economies are visiting there themselves, to find the answers they need among the Spanish, who solved the same problems not so very long ago.

But if the 20th century has finally come to Spain, the landscape, the castles and cathedrals, the cities and towns have hardly changed a bit. What has changed is the official promotions of the Spanish Tourist Office. For a generation or more ads and posters encouraging visitors to Spain have always had two things in common: golden sunshine and girls in bikinis. Now that has all been swept away. The sun is still evident, but the girls are just as likely to be dressed in traditional costumes and the countryside is revealed as lush and green. Best of all, they are calling attention to cathedrals, convents and former mosques, great art collections, charming villages and, yes, castles in Spain. After all, the sun shines everywhere and girls wear bikinis the world over. But the message now is that Spain is as alive today as it was a thousand years ago. The reality of the message is that it is probably more alive now than it ever has been.

Facing page: the fairytale Alcázar of Segovia.

Below: the Gothic cathedral in Segovia (these pages), Old Castile (overleaf). This, the "lady of Spanish cathedrals," was built between 1525 and 1593 on the highest spot in the town. Its position rivals that of the Alcázar (right). The castle in existence today is a reconstruction of the original which dated from the fourteenth century, but which burned in 1862. Bottom right: the Roman Aqueduct, built nearly 2,000 years ago and one of two of the largest surviving Roman structures in the country.

Above and below left: Madrid's Parque del Retiro, whose centerpiece is a large lake, overlooked by the grandiose Monument to Alfonso XII (facing page top). Above left: the Plaza de la Cibeles and Madrid Post Office, and (left) the Royal Palace, near the Plaza de Oriente. The latter, the largest square in central Madrid, contains forty-four statues of Visigothic and Spanish kings and queens (below). Facing page bottom: Madrid's Puerta de Alcalá, built in 1778 on the orders of Charles III. Overleaf: high noon in Toledo on the Río Tajo.

Below and bottom left: Castro-Urdiales, where a fourteenth-century Gothic church, Neustra Señora de la Asunción, commands the town's highest point. This port, which lies to the east of Santander, is thought to be the oldest settlement on Spain's north shore. The rugged coastline (left), renowned for being particularly wild and beautiful, is one of the attractions that have made Castro-Urdiales a seaside resort. Below left: the harbor at Santander in Old Castile. Santander has been an important port since Roman times and, despite explosions, fires and hurricanes in its history, has remained significant as such to the present day. Overleaf: framed by wild rape seed and stray wheat ears, a river and a road slice through cultivated land in La Rioja, the world-famous wine-producing region of northern Spain. Spain has the greatest area under vines of any country on earth and its stable climate gives it a distinct advantage over its rivals in wine-making. Of all the regions, La Rioja is thought to be the best, producing a wine that graces some of the finest cellars in Europe.

These pages and overleaf: the foothills of the Pyrenees, a range of mountains whose peaks mark the border between Spain and France. As Spain was neutral during the Second World War, these mountain villages meant freedom for Allied airmen shot down over occupied France. They would aim to reach the Pyrenees, with the aid of the French Resistance, and progress through Spain to Portugal and the Atlantic. Facing page top: Planoles, near La Molina, (facing page bottom and below) the Serra del Boumort region, just south of the republic of Andorra in the Pyrenees, and (right) the village of Alp. Below right: Oliana, and (overleaf) the Sallent de Gállego, part of a mountain game reserve.

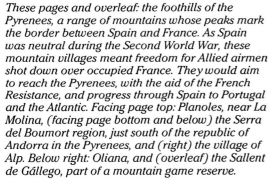

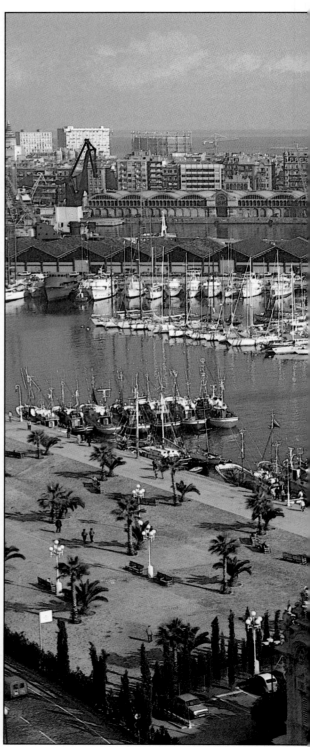

Barcelona (these pages), the second largest city in Spain and one of the
most important ports on the Mediterranean, is a great international city,
renowned for its architecture, its cultural treasures and its sense of style.
A feature here is Las Ramblas, a collection of wide avenues lined with
plane trees (below left), the first of which was constructed over a dry
riverbed. For centuries, these avenues, full of book and flower stalls and
cafés, have been the heart of the city. Barcelona, as the capital of the
most populous province in Spain, Catalonia, is at the center of Catalan
separatism; here Catalan is spoken, albeit that Castilan is the official
language of Spain. Below: Barcelona Harbor, the hub of this, the leading
industrial and commercial center of the country. Bottom left: Barcelona
from Montjuich Hill, on the northwest slopes of which lies a large park.
The hill, which is nearly 700 feet high, slopes steeply away to the sea. Its
summit, reached by cableway, affords a full view of the surrounding
area. Not surprisingly, castles have been built here, the first in 1640.

31

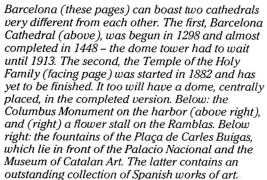

Barcelona (these pages) can boast two cathedrals very different from each other. The first, Barcelona Cathedral (above), was begun in 1298 and almost completed in 1448 – the dome tower had to wait until 1913. The second, the Temple of the Holy Family (facing page) was started in 1882 and has yet to be finished. It too will have a dome, centrally placed, in the completed version. Below: the Columbus Monument on the harbor (above right), and (right) a flower stall on the Ramblas. Below right: the fountains of the Plaça de Carles Buigas, which lie in front of the Palacio Nacional and the Museum of Catalan Art. The latter contains an outstanding collection of Spanish works of art.

The Costa Brava – the Wild Coast – is Spain's most northerly stretch of Mediterranean coastline and some 125 miles long. Three destinations are particularly well known to thousands of holidaymakers for their fine beaches and rugged cliffs: Lloret de Mar (left and bottom left), Tossa de Mar (below) and Calella de Palafugell (below left). Prior to Spain's tourist boom, the former two were quiet fishing villages; today they are white with highrise hotels and, during the season, rich with sunseekers.

Mallorca (these pages), the largest Balearic island, is renowned throughout the world for its sunny climate, superb bathing beaches and relaxing atmosphere. Facing page top and below right: Puerto de Pollensa, (facing page bottom) Palma, the island's capital, (above right) Puerto de Sóller and (below) Formentor cliffs. Above: a windmill near Santa Maria and (right) a horse and cart on a farm at Santañi – both sights characteristic of the Mallorcan countryside.

Menorca is the second largest island in the Balearics and its capital, Mahon (below left), one of the best natural harbors in the Mediterranean. The English admiral, Lord Nelson, lived here for a while when the island was in British hands. Below: Benibeca Vell and (left) Cala Galdana, two resorts on the south coast of Menorca, and (above left) Fornells, a Menorcan port that rivals Mahon in importance. Above: the gold cliffs at Portinatx, on the northern tip of Ibiza, another Balearic island, and (facing page) Ibiza town by night and day.

Facing page top and overleaf: the major tourist center of Benidorm on the east coast of Spain, south of Calpe (facing page bottom). Calpe remains a quiet fishing village, similar to the type of place Benidorm once was. Above, above right, below right and below: Peñíscola, also on the east coast. Lying on a promontory, Peñíscola was always an ideal strategic site for a castle, the first of which was built by the Moors during their occupation of Spain between the eighth and twelfth centuries. The present fortress was constructed by the Knights Templar in the fourteenth century. Right: Altea, considered to be the most beautiful coastal town in Valencia.

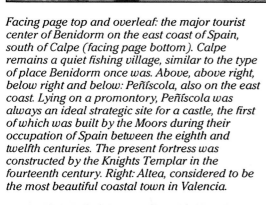

The province of Almeria contains some surprising contrasts. Within the space of a few miles, one can experience the perpetual snows of the eastern half of the Sierra Nevada (below right and bottom right) and then the searing heat of the desert region (below) at the foot of the Sierra Alhamilla. Right: traditional ceramics reflect the colors of the earth and sky in Purullena in the Guadix area and (overleaf) poppies aflame on Andalusian agricultural land near the Sierra Nevada, north of Granada.

48

*Below: Granada seen from the Moorish Alhambra (remaining pictures),
which comprises three groups of buildings: the original eleventh-century
fortress called the Alcazaba, the fourteenth-century Royal Palace, with its
tranquil Portal Gardens (left and bottom left) and the civilized and
elegant Court of Lions (below left), and the simple fourteenth-century
Generalife Palace. The Royal Palace boasts a fantastically ornate interior
– the zenith of Moorish art in Spain – and has become world famous.*

49

Facing page: (top) the rugged coast of Almuñecar on the Costa del Sol and (bottom) nearby Salobreña, the focal point of which is a ruined Moorish castle, surrounded by the remains of a medieval wall. For most of their history, the Spanish of this region feared the sun and the sea, since the sun dried up the rivers and parched the land, while the sea brought marauding pirates. The past decades have seen these historical "curses" turned into million-dollar assets. This Mediterranean coastline has experienced holiday resort development on an unprecedented scale, as northern European sunseekers discovered the pleasures of a holiday with reliably good weather and economically priced accommodation, and Spanish entrepreneurs took the opportunity to provide them with such. Right: the Málaga waterfront in southern Spain. Málaga is renowned as a resort throughout the world, its sun and sand attracting thousands of visitors every year. It has more of interest than a fine beach, though, boasting five beautiful, lavishly decorated churches. Below: flanked by palms and laced with the watery reflections of another gloriously sunny day, expensive yachts fill the exclusive yacht harbor in Marbella known as Puerto José Banus.

Below left: Olvera in southern Spain, where the houses resemble those of Setenil (bottom left) and Torre Alháquime (below), set amid the golden fields of summer to the east of Olvera. This region still retains the simple architecture of an arid land, reminiscent of that brought to Andalusia by the Moors over a thousand years ago. Not surprisingly, many present-day Arabs choose to vacation in this region. As one Lebanese businessman said, "The Spanish people are a warm people, not stiff and formal like many Europeans. The food is much like ours, so is the shape of the houses and towns. To an Arab – well, Andalusia feels like home." Olvera is set on a hill crowned by the ruins of a medieval fortress whose keep and walls can still be seen. One of Cadiz's "white towns," it has a reputation for producing fine saddlery, harness and other such leather goods. Left: the church at Archidona, a town to the east of Antequera in Andalusia which dates from Phoenican times. Overleaf: the view from Mijas, a village snug in the hills above Fuengirola, Andalusia.

Córdoba (these pages), in Andalusia, is one of the best known cities in all Spain. Once it was among the most splendid cities in the western world; between 711 and 1031, the Arabs made it the center of an empire that stretched as far north as the Pyrenees. Over half a million people lived here in a metropolis that could boast 300 mosques, a complete irrigation system for both Córdoba and the surrounding countryside, free schools, universities, public libraries and hospitals – all this while northern Europe was still enduring the Dark Ages. The great Mosque (right and below) for which Córdoba is renowned was built at that time and, as the principal mosque of western Islam, became a center of Arab pilgrimage. It is the only mosque with a Christian church built within it – a decision made in the sixteenth century which, even at the time, was against the wishes of Córdoba's citizens because of the destruction of much of the fabulous interior that it entailed. Facing page bottom: the 800-foot-long Roman bridge across the Guadalquivir, the foundations of which were built after Caesar's defeat of Pompey in 46 BC. Always an important structure, the bridge was rebuilt by the Moors.

Facing page: (top) the Plaza de Espana in Seville, where stands the Palacio Español, part of a complex built for the 1929-30 Ibero-American Exhibition. The complex included the Pabellón Mudéjar (bottom) in the Plaza de América. Seville, Spain's fourth largest city and the capital of Andalusia, lies on a curve in the Guadalquivir River. Its history stretches back over 2,000 years; the town was captured by Julius Caesar in 45 BC and later two Roman emperors, Hadrian and Trajan, were born in the vicinity. Below: a skilled venenciador pours the world-renowned fortified wine known as sherry at the Bodega Terry (right), one of the major cellars in Puerto de Santa Maria. This was the main port for shipments of sherry from Jerez until a railway was extended to Cádiz (above right and below right). Above: bulls bred for fighting in the bullring graze in the countryside around Cádiz known as the Route de Torres. These animals wander at will across the grasslands, watched over by mounted herdsmen who carry long, steel-tipped staffs with which to guide them and keep them at bay – a necessary precaution since the bulls are potentially lethal.

Although vegetation is sparse around Spain's highest peak, Pico de Teide (facing page top) on Tenerife, this, the largest island in the Canaries, boasts valleys lush enough to produce tropical fruits such as bananas, early tomatoes and vegetables. The 12,162-foot-high summit, like most of Tenerife's mountains, is volcanic in origin. There are seven main islands in the archipelago, which lies off the west coast of Africa just north of the Tropic of Cancer. Facing page bottom: pedaloes out of reach of the waves at Playos de Américas in Tenerife. It was here, on the largest of the Canary Islands, that Columbus stopped to take on supplies before crossing the Atlantic for the first time. Today, Playos de Américas is one of the island's prime holiday destinations. Below: colorful fishing craft and sedate pleasure cruisers tie up together at Los Christianos harbor, the centerpiece of Tenerife's most popular winter resort. Left: camels in the volcanic landscape of Timanfaya, and (overleaf) salt pans at sunset at Janubio, both on the island of Lanzarote, the most easterly of the seven. Following page: sunrise over the mighty cliffs of Gran Canaria, the third largest island in the Canaries archipelago and one of the loveliest.

61